Contents

FULL INDONESIAN STIR FRY

Prep Time: 15 mins - **Total Time:** 35 mins

SERVINGS: 4

NUTRITIONAL VALUE

Calories 733.1, Fat 40.6g , Cholesterol 164.5mg , Sodium 1231.8mg , Carbohydrates 55.1g , Protein 42.6g

INGREDIENTS

- 2 (3 oz.) packages ramen noodles (any
- cooking spray
- flavor, discard flavor packet)
- FOR SAUCE
- 2 C. cooked chicken breasts (cut into
- 2 tbsp sambal oelek, or sriracha
- strips)
- 2 tbsp rice vinegar
- 1 C. carrot, cut into matchstick sized
- 2 tbsp sugar
- pieces
- 2 tbsp soy sauce
- 1/4 lb fresh sugar snap pea, trimmed
- 3 tbsp water
- and string removed
- 1 tsp lime juice

- 5 scallions, sliced
- 1 tsp Thai fish sauce
- 1 C. peanuts, chopped (divided)
- 1/4 tsp sesame oil
- 1 (14 oz.) cans bean sprouts, rinsed and
- 1 tbsp cornstarch
- drained
- 1 tsp minced garlic
- 2 eggs
- 2 tbsp oil

DIRECTIONS

Step 1

Break each ramen noodle square into 4 portions.

Step 2

In a pan of the salted boiling water, cook the noodles for about 2-3 minutes.

Step 3

Drain the noodles and rinse under cold water. Again, drain well.

Step 4

In a bowl, add all the sauce ingredients and mix till well combined.

Step 5

Heat a large greased skillet on medium-high heat.

Step 6

Break the eggs and cook till just cooked, stirring continuously.

Step 7

Transfer the scrambled eggs into a plate and keep aside.

Step 8

With the paper towels, wipe out the skillet. Full Indonesian Stir Fry

Step 9

In the same skillet, heat the cooking oil and stir fry the carrots and sugar snap peas for about 2-3 minutes.

Step10

Add the scallions and 2/3 of the peanuts and stir fry for about 1 minute.

Step 11

Add bean sprouts and garlic and stir fry for about 1 minute.

Step 12

With a spoon, push all ingredients to the outside edges of the skillet.

Step 13

Add the ramen noodles and Stir fry for about 1 minute.

Step 14

Add the chicken and sauce mixture and cook till heated through.

Step 15

Stir in the scrambled eggs and cook till heated through.

Step 16

Serve with a topping of the remaining peanuts.

JAPANESE RAMEN PIZZAS

Prep Time: 7 mins - **Total Time:** 32 mins

SERVINGS: 4

NUTRITIONAL VALUE

Calories 577.9, Fat 27.6g , Cholesterol 133.1mg , Sodium 1510.0mg , Carbohydrates 50.6g , Protein 31.9g

INGREDIENTS

- 6 oz. ramen noodles, any flavor
- OTHER TOPPINGS
- (discarded seasoning packet)
- black olives (optional)
- 1/2 C. milk
- mushroom (optional)
- 1 egg, beaten
- canned jalapeño slices (optional)
- 1/4 C. Parmesan cheese, grated
- bell pepper (optional)
- 1 C. barbecue sauce (of your choice)
- red pepper flakes (optional)
- 1 C. cooked chicken, chopped
- 1/2 red onion, sliced thinly
- 11 oz. mandarin oranges, drained well
- 2 C. mozzarella cheese, grated

DIRECTIONS

Step 1

Set your oven to 350 degrees F before doing anything else and line a pizza pan with a greased piece of foil.

Step 2

In a pan of the salted boiling water, cook the ramen noodles for about 2-3 minutes.

Step 3

Drain the noodles.

Step 4

Meanwhile in a bowl, add egg, milk and Parmesan cheese and beat till well combined.

Step 5

Add the noodles and stir to combined. Place the noodle mixture onto prepared pan evenly.

Step 6

Cook in the oven for about 10 minutes.

Step 7

Remove pan from the oven and spread barbecue sauce over noodles, followed by the chicken, onions and oranges.

Step 8

Sprinkle with the mozzarella cheese evenly.

Step 9

Cook in the oven for about 10-15 minutes.

Step10

Remove from the oven and keep aside for about 5 minutes before slicing.

SWEET THAI TILAPIA

Prep Time: 15 mins - **Total Time:** 30 mins

SERVINGS: 4

NUTRITIONAL VALUE

Calories 232.3, Fat 7.9g , Cholesterol 46.8mg , Sodium 526.8mg , Carbohydrates 18.6g , Protein 21.7g

INGREDIENTS

- 2 1/2 oz. ramen noodles, broken into
- 3 tilapia fillets, cut in chunks
- pieces
- 1 tbsp oil
- 1 red bell pepper, cut in strips
- breadcrumbs, for fish
- 1 green bell pepper, cut in strips
- 1 medium onion, cut in strips
- 2 tbsp sweet Thai sweet chili sauce

DIRECTIONS

Step 1

Prepare the ramen noodles according to package's directions.

Step 2

Drain the noodles and keep aside.

Step 3

Heat a lightly greased skillet and and sauté the peppers and onions till soft.

Step 4

Add the noodles and stir to combine.

Step 5

Coat the tilapia chunks with the breadcrumbs evenly.

Step 6

In a deep fryer, heat the oil to 350 degrees and fry the tilapia chunks till golden.

Step 7

Transfer the tilapia chunks onto a paper towel lined plate to drain

Step 8

Add tilapia chunks and chili sauce into the noodle mixture and stir to combine.

INUTE SHIBUYA RAMEN

Prep Time: 10 mins - **Total Time:** 10 mins

SERVINGS: 1

NUTRITIONAL VALUE

Calories 602.8, Fat 35.1g , Cholesterol 200.6mg , Sodium 4094.5mg , Carbohydrates 11.8g , Protein 56.8g

INGREDIENTS

- 1 (3 oz.) packages chicken-flavored
- 1/4 C. cheddar cheese, grated
- ramen noodles
- 1 C. water
- 3 -4 thin turkey slices, cut into bite
- sized pieces

DIRECTIONS

Step 1

In a pan, add 1 C. of the water and noodles and bring to a boil.

Step 2

Place the turkey pieces over the noodles and remove from the heat.

Step 3

Add seasoning packet and stir to combine well.

Step 4

Sprinkle with the cheese and keep aside, covered till the cheese is melted.

Step 5

Serve immediately.

TIPSY MAHI MAHI TERIYAKI WITH FRUITY JALAPENO SALSA

Prep Time: 45 mins - **Total Time:** 55 mins

SERVINGS: 4

NUTRITIONAL VALUE

Calories 324.5, Fat 8.4g , Cholesterol 8.4g , Sodium 148.9mg , Carbohydrates 1297.8mg , Protein 17.4g

INGREDIENTS

DIRECTIONS

Step 1

To make the salsa:

- 1 large ripe mango

Step 2

Peel the mango and cut it into 1/4 inch

- 1/4 C. finely chopped red onion
- dices.

- 1 tbsp vegetable oil

Step 3

Get a serving bowl: Toss it in the mango

- 1 tbsp fresh lime juice
- dices with the rest of the ingredients. Place 1 tbsp finely chopped of fresh mint
- it in the fridge until ready to serve.
- 1 tsp minced jalapeno pepper, with

Step 4

To make the mahi mahi fillets:

- seeds

Step 5

Get a small bowl: Mix in it the soy sauce, 1/4 tsp kosher salt

- sweet sake, vegetable oil, light brown
- Marinade:
- sugar, fresh ginger, and minced garlic to
- 1/4 C. soy sauce
- make the marinade.
- 1/4 C. sweet sake

Step 6

Get a large zip lock bag: Place in it the 1 tbsp vegetable oil

- mahi mahi fillets and marinade. Seal it
- 1 tbsp light brown sugar
- and shake it to coat. Place it in the fridge

- 1 tsp grated fresh ginger
- for 28 min.
- 1 tsp minced garlic
- 4 mahi mahi fillets, about 6 oz. each

Step 7

Before you do anything preheat the grill

- and 1 inch thick
- and grease it.
- vegetable oil

Step 8

Drain the mahi mahi fillet. Spray them

- on both sides with a cooking spray. Cook
- them in the grill for 4 to 6 min on each
- side.

Step 9

Serve your teriyaki mahi mahi fillets with the jalapeno salsa.

Step10

Enjoy.

SHERRY CHINESE TERIYAKI MEAT

Prep Time: 15 mins - **Total Time:** 25 mins

SERVINGS: 10

NUTRITIONAL VALUE

Calories 980.7, Fat 96.5g , Cholesterol 134.8mg , Sodium 995.8mg , Carbohydrates 12.3g , Protein 12.4g

INGREDIENTS

- 3 -4 lbs beef or 3 -4 lbs chicken
- 1 inch piece ginger, crushed
- Sauce:
- 3 green onions (chopped fine)
- 2/3 C. shoyu (Asian soy sauce)
- 1 tsp Chinese five spice powder (optional)
- 1/2 C. sugar
- 2 tbsp sherry wine or 2 tbsp white wine
- 3 garlic cloves, minced

DIRECTIONS

Step 1

Get a large zip lock bag: Combine in it all the ingredients. Seal the bag and shake it to coat. Place it in the fridge for 5 h to an overnight.

Step 2

Before you do anything preheat the oven to 325 F.

Step 3

Pour the mix into a roasting casserole dish. Cook it in the oven for 1 h 10 min. Serve your meat casserole warm.

Step 4

Enjoy.

HEALTHY JUICY TERIYAKI TUNA STEAKS

Prep Time: 2 hrs - **Total Time:** 2 hrs 12 mins

SERVINGS: 4

NUTRITIONAL VALUE

Calories 179.4, Fat 10.1g , Cholesterol 0.0mg , Sodium 1011.1mg , Carbohydrates 14.2g , Protein 2.1g

INGREDIENTS

- 1/4 C. soy sauce
- 1 tsp ground ginger
- 3 tbsp brown sugar
- 1/8 tsp black pepper
- 3 tbsp olive oil
- 4 tuna steaks (about 6 oz. each)
- 2 tbsp white wine vinegar
- 2 tbsp sherry wine or 2 tbsp chicken
- broth
- 2 tbsp unsweetened pineapple juice
- 3 cloves garlic, minced

DIRECTIONS

Step 1

Get a large mixing bowl: Mix in it all the ingredients except for the tuna steaks to make the marinade.

Step 2

Get a large zip lock bag: Place in it the tuna steaks with marinade. Seal it and shake it to coat. Place it in the fridge for 1 h 20 min.

Step 3

Before you do anything preheat the grill and grease it.

Step 4

Remove the tuna steaks from the marinade and grill them for 7 min on each side while basting them with the marinade.

Step 5

Serve your steaks warm.

Step 6

Enjoy.

CHICKEN KABOBS II

Prep Time: 1 hr 30 mins **- Total Time:** 2 hrs

SERVINGS: 24

NUTRITIONAL VALUE

Calories 93.7, Fat 5.0g , Cholesterol 31.4mg , Sodium 717.1mg , Carbohydrates 3.0g , Protein 8.5g

INGREDIENTS

- MARINADE
- 2 lbs boneless skinless chicken thighs
- 15 oz teriyaki sauce
- 1 tbsp sesame seeds, toasted
- 6 tbsp sesame oil

- 1/4 tsp minced garlic
- 1 lemon, juice of
- 1 tbsp Splenda granular (sugar substitute)

DIRECTIONS

Step 1

Place some bamboo skewers in some water to some for at least 1 h 10 min.

Step 2

Get a large mixing bowl: Combine in it all the marinade ingredients and whisk them well.

Step 3

Cut the chicken thighs into stripes and dip them into the marinade. Cover the bowl with a piece of foil and place it in the fridge for 1 h 30 min.

Step 4

Before you do anything preheat the oven to 375 F.

Step 5

Thread each chicken thigh strip into a bamboo skewer. Lay them on a lined up baking sheet. Cook them in the oven for 32 min.

Step 6

Sprinkle the sesame seeds over the skewers. Serve them warm.

Step 7

Enjoy.

TILAPIA FILLETS WITH TERIYAKI SAUCE

Prep Time: 5 mins - **Total Time:** 15 mins

SERVINGS: 5

NUTRITIONAL VALUE

Calories 245.6, Fat 4.8g , Cholesterol 62.5mg , Sodium 1680.0mg , Carbohydrates 23.3g , Protein 28.1g

INGREDIENTS

- 1 tbsp oil
- 1 tsp fresh ginger, grated
- 5 tilapia fillets
- 1/2 tsp garlic, minced
- 1/2 C. brown sugar
- 1/4 C. seasoned rice wine vinegar
- 1/2 C. soy sauce

DIRECTIONS

Step 1

Place a large skillet over medium heat. Add the oil and heat it. Lay in it the tilapia Fillets.

Step 2

Get a mixing bowl: Mix in it the remaining ingredients to make the sauce. Pour the sauce all over the tilapia. Cook them until the fish is done and sauce is thick.

Step 3

Serve your tilapia fillets with teriyaki sauce warm.

Step 4

Enjoy.

GLAZED SALMON FILLETS WITH ORZO

Prep Time: 15 mins - **Total Time:** 25 mins

SERVINGS: 4

NUTRITIONAL VALUE

Calories 849.7, Fat 31.3g , Cholesterol 153.6mg , Sodium 3001.4mg , Carbohydrates 55.8g , Protein 81.8g

INGREDIENTS

- 4 salmon fillets (2 lbs total)
- 2 tbsp olive oil, combined with garlic
- 1 oz canola oil
- 1/2 C. red bell pepper, diced
- 1 oz soy sauce
- 1/3 C. parmesan cheese
- 8 oz teriyaki sauce
- 8 oz spinach, julienned
- 8 oz orzo pasta, precooked
- 2 garlic cloves, minced

DIRECTIONS

Step 1

Before you do anything preheat the grill and grease it.

Step 2

Coat the salmon fillets with soy sauce and brush them with the oil. Cook them in the grill for 4 min on each side.

Step 3

Brush the salmon fillets with 2 oz of teriyaki glaze. Cook them for 3 min on each side.

Step 4

Cook the orzo according to the directions on the package.

Step 5

Place a large skillet over medium heat. Heat the oil in it. Add the garlic with peppers and orzo. Cook them for 2 min.

Step 6

Stir in the cheese until it melts. Turn off the heat and add the spinach. Stir them several times until the spinach wilts.

Step 7

Serve your orzo with the glazed salmon fillets and the remaining teriyaki sauce.

Step 8

Enjoy.

NUTTY TERIYAKI BURGES

Prep Time: 30mins - **Total Time:** 45 mins

SERVINGS: 4

NUTRITIONAL VALUE

Calories 402.7, Fat 11.1g, Cholesterol 93.0mg, Sodium 31740.4mg, Carbohydrates 62.8g, Protein 213.5g

INGREDIENTS

- 1/2 tbsp peanut oil
- 1/4 C. soy sauce
- 1/2 C. onion (purple)
- 1/4 C. teriyaki sauce
- 1 C. zucchini

- 1/4 C. walnut pieces
- 1/2 C. red bell pepper
- 1 1/2 C. brown rice (cooked)
- 2 eggs
- 1/2 tsp ginger (ground)
- 1/2 tsp cumin

DIRECTIONS

Step 1

Before you do anything heat the oven on 350 F.

Step 2

Chop the bell pepper with zucchini until they become fine. Mince the onion.

Step 3

Place a large skillet on medium heat. Add the oil and heat it. Stir in the onion and cook it for 6 min.

Step 4

Stir in the chopped zucchini with bell pepper to the onion. Cook them for 16 min while stirring occasionally. Turn off the heat and allow the mix to lose heat.

Step 5

Get a mixing bowl: Add the eggs and beat them. Stir in the onion mix with ginger, cumin, soy sauce, teriyaki sauce, walnuts and cooked rice. Mix them well. Shape the mix into 4 burgers.

Step 6

Place the burgers on the baking pan. Cook them in the oven for 8 min on each side.

Step 7

Assemble your burgers with your favorite toppings. Serve them right away.

Step 8

Enjoy.

JAPANESE FRUITY CHICKEN CURRY

Prep Time: 10 mins - **Total Time:** 55 mins

SERVINGS: 4

NUTRITIONAL VALUE

Calories 420.5, Fat 17.9g , Cholesterol 101.1mg , Sodium 734.0mg , Carbohydrates 33.1g , Protein 31.9g

INGREDIENTS

DIRECTIONS

- 3 C. chicken stock

Step 1

Place a medium saucepan over medium

- 1 tbsp canola oil
- heat: Pour the stock in it and heat it
- 1 lb boneless skinless chicken, cut into
- through.
- chunks

Step 2

Sprinkle some salt and pepper on the

- salt and pepper
- chicken.
- 3 tbsp butter

Step 3

Place a large skillet over medium heat: Heat 1 tsp fresh ginger, finely chopped

- the oil in it. Add the chicken pieces and
- 1/2 medium onion, finely chopped
- cook them for 5 min on each side. Drain it
- 1/2 medium onion, cut into 1-inch chunks
- and place it aside.
- 1 garlic clove, finely chopped

Step 4

Add the butter to the skillet and heat it 3 tbsp flour

- until it melts. Cook in it the ginger, garlic, 2 tbsp curry powder
- and chopped onion for 4 min.
- 2 tbsp crushed tomatoes

Step 5

Add the flour and cook them for 2 min. Stir 1 bay leaf

- in 1/2 C. of hot stock and mix them well.
- 1 medium carrot, chopped to 1/2-inch
- Stir in the tomato with curry.
- pieces

Step 6

Transfer the mix to the pot with the

- 1 medium potato, chopped in 1-inch
- remaining hot stock. Stir in the chicken,
- pieces

- onion, potato, and carrot.
- 1 small fuji apple, grated
- 1 tsp honey

Step 7

Cook the curry until it starts simmering.

- 1 tbsp soy sauce
- Cook it for 32 min. Stir in the apples, soy
- sauce, and honey.

Step 8

Cook the curry for 6 min. Serve it warm

- with some rice.

Step 9

Enjoy.

JAPANESE CROCK STEW

Prep Time: 5 mins - **Total Time:** 12 hrs 5 mins

SERVINGS: 6

NUTRITIONAL VALUE

Calories 361.5, Fat 6.9g , Cholesterol 96.7mg , Sodium 1217.1mg , Carbohydrates 33.6g , Protein 36.8g

INGREDIENTS

- 2 lbs beef stew meat
- 3 medium potatoes, peeled and chopped
- 1 C. water

- 1 white onion, diced
- 1/2 C. Japanese sake
- 1/4 C. sugar
- 1/4 C. soy sauce
- 1 tsp salt
- 1/2 lb baby carrots

DIRECTIONS

Step 1

Stir all the ingredients into a crockpot. Put on the lid and cook the stew for 11 h on low or 5 h on high.

Step 2

Serve your stew warm.

Step 3

Enjoy.

JAPANESE JUICY BURGERS

Prep Time: 15 mins - **Total Time:** 25 mins

SERVINGS: 4

NUTRITIONAL VALUE

Calories 404.4, Fat 20.2g , Cholesterol 125.7mg , Sodium 548.5mg , Carbohydrates 26.8g , Protein 27.1g

INGREDIENTS

- 1 lb ground beef
- vegetable oil, for frying

- 1/2 onion, chopped
- 3 tbsp ketchup
- 1 egg
- 3 tbsp Worcestershire sauce
- 1/4 C. milk
- 1 C. panko breadcrumbs
- pepper

DIRECTIONS

Step 1

Place a large skillet over medium heat. Heat the oil in it. Cook in it the onion for 3 min.

Step 2

Get a large mixing bowl: Add the milk with egg and whisk them well. Stir in the breadcrumbs and place them aside.

Step 3

Get a large mixing bowl: Combine in it the beef with onion, breadcrumbs mix, a pinch of salt and pepper. Mix them well. Shape the mix into 4 patties.

Step 4

Place a large skillet over medium heat. Heat some oil in it. Cook in it the burger patties for 4 min. Flip them.

Step 5

Pour 1/4 C. of hot water into the skillet. Put on the lid and coo the patties for 4 min. Remove the lid after all the water evaporates.

Step 6

Place the burger patties aside. Stir the ketchup and Worcestershire sauce into the skillet. Mix them well and heat them to make the sauce.

Step 7

Drizzle the sauce all over the burgers then serve them warm.

Step 8

Enjoy.

JAPANESE CRUSTED POTATO BITES

Prep Time: 30 mins - **Total Time:** 30 mins

SERVINGS: 4

NUTRITIONAL VALUE

Calories 231.9, Fat 2.8g , Cholesterol 33.1mg , Sodium 461.1mg , Carbohydrates 44.6g , Protein 7.3g

INGREDIENTS

- 3 -4 C. leftover mashed potatoes
- 1 C. panko breadcrumbs
- 1 C. corn
- oil(for frying)
- 1/2 C. flour
- 1 egg, beaten

DIRECTIONS

Step 1

Get a mixing bowl: Add the corn with potato. Combine them well. Shape the mix into patties.

Step 2

Dust the potato patties with flour, dip them in the beaten egg and coat them with the panko crumbs.

Step 3

Heat the oil in a large pan. Cook in it the potato patties until they become golden brown. Serve your potato bites warm.

Step 4

Enjoy.

CRUNCHY JAPANESE RAMEN

Prep Time: 5 mins - **Total Time:** 15 mins

SERVINGS: 2

NUTRITIONAL VALUE

Calories 377.9, Fat 22.6g , Cholesterol 0.0mg , Sodium 881.3mg , Carbohydrates 39.1g , Protein 6.3g

INGREDIENTS

- 1 package ramen noodles
- 1 tsp sesame oil
- 2 C. thinly sliced cabbage
- soy sauce
- 1 C. thinly sliced onion
- 2 tbsp cooking oil, divided
- 1 tsp ginger powder

DIRECTIONS

Step 1

Cook the ramen noodles according to the directions on the package. Drain it

Step 2

Place a large pan over medium heat. Heat 1 tbsp of oil in it. Cook in it the onion with cabbage for 4 to 6 min.

Step 3

Add the noodles with the remaining oil. Cook them for 2 min. Stir in the rest of the ingredients. Cook them for 2 min. Serve your noodles warm.

Step 4

Enjoy.

JAPANESE RUSSET CURRY

Prep Time: 10 mins - **Total Time:** 25 mins

SERVINGS: 4

NUTRITIONAL VALUE

Calories 292.4, Fat 9.0g , Cholesterol 0.0mg , Sodium 57.8mg , Carbohydrates 50.3g , Protein 9.9g

INGREDIENTS

- 2 tbsp oil
- 1 (14 1/2 oz) cans baby corn, cut in half
- 1 1/2 C. chicken
- 1 (3 1/2 oz) boxes golden curry sauce
- 1 onion, diced
- mix
- 1 large russet potato, peeled, in bite-
- size cubes
- 1 head broccoli, cut into small pieces

DIRECTIONS

Step 1

Place a soup pot over medium heat. Heat the oil in it. Cook it in the chicken with onion for 5 min.

Step 2

Add the potato with 2 3/4 C. of water. Put on the lid and lower the heat. Cook them for 12 min. Crumble the curry sauce mix and stir it until it melts for 3 min.

Step 3

Stir in the corn with broccoli. Cook the stew for 4 min. Serve it warm.

Step 4

Enjoy.

JAPANESE BELL RICE OMELET

Prep Time: 20 mins **- Total Time:** 45 mins

SERVINGS: 4

NUTRITIONAL VALUE

Calories 692.1, Fat 36.0g , Cholesterol 397.5mg , Sodium 683.6mg , Carbohydrates 67.3g , Protein 22.8g

INGREDIENTS

- 4 C. cooked rice
- 8 eggs
- 100 g carrots, chopped in very small
- 2 tsp sugar
- pieces
- 2 tsp oil
- 100 g red capsicums, chopped in very
- salt and pepper

- small pieces
- 4 tsp oil, to cook eggs, using one tsp at a time 100 g onions, chopped in very small
- 8 tsp tomato ketchup, garnish
- pieces
- 150 g turkey bacon, chopped in small
- batons
- 50 g tomato paste
- 2 tsp oil

DIRECTIONS

Step 1

Get a large mixing bowl: Toss in it the veggies with bacon. Place them aside.

Step 2

Get a mixing bowl: Beat in it the eggs with sugar, oil, salt and pepper. Place the mix aside.

Step 3

Heat 2 tsp of oil in a deep pan and cook in it the veggies mix for 8 min. Stir in the rice with tomato paste. Mix them well and cook them for 3 min.

Step 4

Place a large no sticking pan over medium heat. Heat 1 tsp of oil in it Spread 1/4 f the egg mix in it to coat the pan and cook it for 3 min.

Step 5

Release the egg sheet from the side of the pan with a spatula. Place 1/4 of the rice mix on the center of 1 side of the egg sheet.

Step 6

Cover the rice with the second side of the egg sheet. Cover the pan with a serving plate and flip it. Place it aside and repeat the process with the rest of the ingredients.

Step 7

Serve your omelet with your favorite toppings.

Step 8

Enjoy.

JAPANESE BAKED SWEET POTATO

Prep Time: 10 mins - **Total Time:** 1 hr 10 mins

SERVINGS: 4

NUTRITIONAL VALUE

Calories 147.2, Fat 5.1g , Cholesterol 0.0mg , Sodium 535.3mg , Carbohydrates 23.3g , Protein 2.5g

INGREDIENTS

- 2 tbsp brown sugar
- 1 tbsp toasted sesame seeds
- 3 tbsp low soy sauce
- 1 sheet of toasted nori
- 2 tbsp mirin
- 1 tbsp dark sesame oil
- 4 garlic cloves, minced
- 2 -3 sweet potatoes, diced

DIRECTIONS

Step 1

Before you do anything preheat the oven to 400 F. Grease a casserole dish.

Step 2

Get a mixing bowl: Mix in it all the ingredients except for the potato to make the sauce.

Step 3

Lay potato slices over the casserole dish and drizzle the sauce all over it. Put on the lid then cook it in the oven for 52 min.

Step 4

Drizzle the dripping and the marinade from the casserole dish all over the potato. Remove the cover and cook it in the oven for 12 min.

Step 5

Top your baked potato with sesame seeds and nori. Serve it warm.

Step 6

Enjoy.

JAPANESE CHICKEN THIGHS SKILLET

Prep Time: 10 mins - **Total Time:** 30 mins

SERVINGS: 4

NUTRITIONAL VALUE

Calories 128.4, Fat 7.2g , Cholesterol 39.4mg , Sodium 585.9mg , Carbohydrates 6.1g , Protein 9.6g

INGREDIENTS

- 2 -3 boneless chicken thighs
- japanese sansho pepper (optional)
- 8 fresh shiitake mushrooms
- shichimi togarashi pepper or red chili pepper 8 shishito green peppers or 3 small bell
- flakes (optional)

- peppers
- 2 -3 tbsp mirin
- 2 -3 tbsp soy sauce

DIRECTIONS

Step 1

Discard the fat from the chicken. Discard the mushroom tips and cut them into quarters.

Step 2

Remove the bell peppers stems and cut them into bite size pieces.

Step 3

Place a large skillet over medium heat. Grease it with some oil. Cook in it the chicken thighs with the skin facing down until it becomes crisp and golden brown.

Step 4

Stir in the pepper with mushroom. Flip the chicken thighs and cook them on the other side until they become golden brown.

Step 5

Stir in the mirin with soy sauce. Cook them until they sauce becomes thick, the chicken and veggies done. Serve your chicken skillet warm.

Step 6

Enjoy.

WARM JAPANESE MIRIN EGGPLANTS SALAD

Prep Time: 10 mins **- Total Time:** 30 mins

SERVINGS: 4

NUTRITIONAL VALUE

Calories 368.3, Fat 12.3g , Cholesterol 0.0mg , Sodium 971.9mg , Carbohydrates 64.0g , Protein 12.7g

INGREDIENTS

- 8 Japanese eggplants
- 3 tbsp mirin
- 3 tbsp vegetable oil
- 1 C. water
- 1/4 tsp chili pepper flakes, to taste
- 1 packet dried bonito flakes
- 3 1/2 tbsp soy sauce

DIRECTIONS

Step 1

Score the eggplants with a sharp knife lengthwise after each half inch.

Step 2

Transfer the eggplant with the rest of the ingredients to a heavy saucepan. Cook them until they start simmering.

Step 3

Keep simmering the eggplant mix for 22 min while stirring it from time to time. Serve your eggplant salad.

Step 4

Enjoy..

JAPANESE SHRIMP STEW

Prep Time: 10 mins **- Total Time:** 32 mins

SERVINGS: 2

NUTRITIONAL VALUE

Calories 540.0, Fat 9.9g, Cholesterol 85.1mg, Sodium 1688.5mg, Carbohydrates 87.8g, Protein 22.0g

INGREDIENTS

- 2 1/2 C. dashi stock
- 1 C. japanese short-grain rice, uncooked
- 3 tbsp soy sauce
- 1/2 red pepper
- 2 tbsp mirin
- 12 snow peas, halved on the diagonal
- 1/2 tsp sesame oil
- 16 large shrimp, uncooked
- 1 tbsp canola oil
- 2 spring onions, finely sliced
- 2 tsp finely grated ginger

DIRECTIONS

Step 1

Get a small mixing bowl: Whisk in it the stock, soy sauce, mirin and sesame oil.

Step 2

Place a saucepan over medium heat. Heat the oil in it. Cook in it the green onion for 2 min.

Step 3

Stir in the rice with ginger. Cook them for 2 min. Stir in the stock and sauce mix, red pepper and snow peas. Cook the stew until it starts boiling.

Step 4

Put on the cover and lower the heat. Cook the stew for 17 min. Remove the lid and lay the shrimp on top.

Step 5

Put the lid back on and cook the stew for 6 min. Serve your stew warm.

Step 6

Enjoy.

JAPANESE GREEN BEANS SALAD

Prep Time: 5 mins - **Total Time:** 15 mins

SERVINGS: 4

NUTRITIONAL VALUE

Calories 109.9, Fat 3.6g , Cholesterol 0.0mg , Sodium 801.1mg , Carbohydrates 17.3g , Protein 4.9g

INGREDIENTS

- 500 g fresh green beans
- 2 tbsp yellow sugar
- 3 tbsp sesame seeds
- 1 pinch salt
- 3 tbsp soy sauce

DIRECTIONS

Step 1

Place a pan over medium heat. Toast the sesame seeds in it for 2 min. Transfer it to a pestle and grind it slightly.

Step 2

Get a large mixing bowl: Stir in it the sesame seeds with the soy sauce, sugar, and a pinch of salt. Whisk them well to make the dressing.

Step 3

Trim the green beans. Bring salted saucepan of water to a boil. Cook in it the green beans until they become light green.

Step 4

Remove them from the water and rinse them with some water to lose heat. Drain the and pat them dry.

Step 5

Toss the green beans with the dressing. Serve it.

Step 6

Enjoy.

JAPANESE CHICKEN DRUMSTICKS WITH BARBECUED BEANS AND HOT SLAW

Prep Time: 15 mins - **Total Time:** 1 hr 15 mins

SERVINGS: 4

NUTRITIONAL VALUE

Calories 746.4, Fat 20.5g , Cholesterol 118.2mg , Sodium 1063.7mg , Carbohydrates 109.2g , Protein 37.0g

INGREDIENTS

- 8 chicken drumsticks or 1 1/2-2 lbs
- cooking spray
- chicken drumsticks

- 1/2 head cabbage, cored
- 1 tbsp olive oil
- 1 medium carrot
- 1/4 C. ponzu sauce, lime sauce
- 1 tbsp olive oil
- 1 tbsp ketchup
- 2 tbsp rice vinegar
- 1/2 C. honey
- 2 tbsp pure maple syrup
- 1/2-1 garlic clove, minced
- 1 tbsp sriracha sauce
- salt and pepper
- 1 tbsp lime juice
- 3/4 C. ketchup
- 1/2 tsp ground ginger
- 1/2 C. pure maple syrup
- salt
- 1/2 tbsp liquid smoke flavoring
- 1/2 tsp dry mustard
- 1/4 tsp garlic powder
- salt and pepper
- 1 C. onion, chopped
- 2 C. canned black-eyed peas, drained and

- rinsed

DIRECTIONS

Step 1

To make the chicken drumsticks:

Step 2

Before you do anything preheat the oven to 375 F. Lay the chicken drumsticks in a greased casserole dish.

Step 3

Get a small mixing bowl: Whisk in it the soy sauce, ketchup, honey, garlic, salt and pepper. Drizzle the mix all over the chicken drumsticks.

Step 4

Place the chicken pan in the oven and cook it for 30 min. Flip the chicken drumsticks and cook them for another 30 min. Japanese Chicken Drumsticks with Barbecued Beans and Hot Slaw 45

Step 5

To make the barbecued beans:

Step 6

Place a heavy saucepan over medium heat: Stir in it the ketchup, pure maple syrup, smoke flavoring, mustard powder, garlic powder, salt and pepper. Cook them for 10 min.

Step 7

In the meantime, chop the onion and cook it in a greased pan for 6 min. Transfer the cooked onion with black eyed peas into the saucepan.

Step 8

Put on the lid and coo them until the bean becomes thick.

Step 9

Cut the carrot and cabbage into thin strips.

Step10

To make the hot slaw:

Step 11

Grease a wok or a pan with a cooking spray. Cook in it the carrot and cabbage for 4 min.

Step 12

Get a small bowl: Whisk in it the olive oil, rice vinegar, pure maple syrup, Sriracha Hot Chili sauce, lime juice, ground ginger, salt and pepper to make the dressing.

Step 13

Drizzle the sauce all over the carrot and cabbage mix. Cook them for 3 min.

Step 14

Serve your chicken drumsticks warm with the barbecued beans and warm hot slaw.

Step 15

Enjoy.

JAPANESE CHICKEN SOUP

Prep Time: 10 mins - **Total Time:** 15 mins

SERVINGS: 4

NUTRITIONAL VALUE

Calories 210.7, Fat 5.7g , Cholesterol 125.9mg , Sodium 733.6mg , Carbohydrates 6.3g , Protein 28.0g

INGREDIENTS

- 1 lb ground chicken or 1 lb beef
- flour or starch, as needed
- 1/4 C. miso
- green onion, chopped
- 1/4 C. sake

- 1/4 C. fresh ginger, grated
- 1 egg

DIRECTIONS

Step 1

Get a small bowl: Whisk in it the miso with sake.

Step 2

Get a mixing bowl: Combine in it all the ingredients. Mix them well.

Step 3

Bring some nabe broth to a boil in a large saucepan. Drop the chicken mix using a tbsp into the hot broth and cook them until they are no longer pink.

Step 4

Serve your chicken meatballs soup warm.

Step 5

Enjoy.

CUCUMBER SALAD IN JAPAN

Prep Time: 15 mins - **Total Time:** 45 mins

SERVINGS: 4

NUTRITIONAL VALUE

Calories 55 kcal, Carbohydrates 10.5 g, Cholesterol 0 mg, Fat 1.6 g, Protein 0.8 g, Sodium 111 mg

INGREDIENTS

- 2 tbsps white sugar
- 2 large cucumbers - peeled, seeded, and
- 2 tbsps rice vinegar

- cut into 1/4-inch slices
- 1 tsp Asian (toasted) sesame oil
- 1 tsp chili paste (sambal oelek)
- salt to taste

DIRECTIONS

Step 1

Get a bowl. Mix the following evenly: salt, sugar, chili paste, sesame oil, and rice vinegar.

Step 2

Combine with the wet mixture, your cucumbers, and set the salad to marinade for 35 mins on a countertop.

Step 3

Enjoy the salad at room temp.

HOUSE FRIED RICE II

Prep Time: 15 mins - **Total Time:** 30 mins

SERVINGS: 2

NUTRITIONAL VALUE

Calories 906 kcal, Fat 14.8 g, Carbohydrates 168.2g, Protein 21.9 g, Cholesterol 186 mg, Sodium 1598 mg

INGREDIENTS

- 2 tsp canola oil
- 1 tsp fish sauce
- 2 eggs
- 1 tbsp sriracha sauce

- 1/2 tsp water
- 1/2 tsp white sugar
- 2 tsp sesame oil, divided
- 1/2 tsp salt
- 1/2 onion, diced
- 1/2 tsp ground white pepper
- 1 clove garlic, minced
- 1/2 tsp mono glutamate
- 1/4 C. frozen peas and carrots, thawed
- 1/4 C. chopped green onion, divided
- and patted dry with paper towel
- 1/4 C. chopped fresh cilantro
- 2 C. cold cooked jasmine rice
- 1 cucumber
- 2 tsp light soy sauce

DIRECTIONS

Step 1

In a bowl, add the eggs and water and beat till smooth.

Step 2

In a large skillet, heat 2 tsp of the canola oil on high heat and cook the egg mixture for about 2-3 minutes, stirring continuously. Transfer the cooked eggs into a plate.

Step 3

In the same pan, heat 1 tsp of the sesame oil and enough canola oil that covers the surface of the skillet and sauté the onion and garlic in oil for about 1-2 minutes.

Step 4

Stir in the peas and carrots and cook for about 1-2 minutes. Add the cooked eggs and stir to combine. Slowly, add the rice, breaking the clumps. Cook for abut 2-3 minutes, stirring continuously.

Step 5

Stir in the soy sauce, fish sauce, sriracha sauce, sugar, salt, 1/2 tsp of the white pepper and mono glutamate and cook for about 2-3 minutes.

Step 6

Remove pan from the heat and gently toss in the green onion and cilantro.

Step 7

With a vegetable shredder, peel the outside skin of the cucumber to create a ragged design on the outside.

Step 8

Cut the cucumber into the slices diagonally and arrange in a circle around the serving platter. Place the rice in the middle of the platter.

Step 9

Serve with a topping of the additional green onion and a dash of white pepper.

THAI FRIED RICE

Prep Time: 15 mins - **Total Time:** 45 mins

SERVINGS: 6

NUTRITIONAL VALUE

Calories 352 kcal, Fat 6.1 g, Carbohydrates 56.9g, Protein 17 g, Cholesterol 38 mg, Sodium 409 mg

INGREDIENTS

- 1 1/2 C. uncooked white rice

- 1 lb. boneless chicken meat, cubed
- 3 C. water
- 1 onion, sliced
- 1 tbsp curry powder
- 1 (20 oz.) can pineapple chunks, drained
- 2 tbsp Asian fish sauce
- 2 tbsp pineapple juice
- 1 tbsp vegetable oil

DIRECTIONS

Step 1

In a pan, add the rice and water on high heat and bring to a boil.

Step 2

Reduce the heat to medium-low and simmer, covered for about 20-25 minutes.

Step 3

Remove from the heat and keep aside.

Step 4

In a small bowl, mix together the curry powder, fish sauce and pineapple juice.

Step 5

In a large skillet, heat the vegetable oil on medium-high heat and sear the chicken and onion for about 5 minutes.

Step 6

Stir in the cooked rice, pineapple chunks and curry mixture and cook for about 5-10 minutes.

FILIPINO FRIED RICE

Prep Time: 15 mins - **Total Time:** 45 mins

SERVINGS: 4

NUTRITIONAL VALUE

Calories 239 kcal, Fat 6 g, Carbohydrates 39.8g, Protein 5.7 g, Cholesterol 49 mg, Sodium 482 mg

INGREDIENTS

- 2 C. water
- 1 egg, beaten
- 1 C. uncooked white rice
- 2 tbsp soy sauce
- 1 tsp butter
- 1 tbsp sesame oil
- 1 small onion, minced
- 1 large clove garlic, minced
- 1 tsp diced chile pepper

DIRECTIONS

Step 1

In a pan, add the rice and water and bring to a boil.

Step 2

Reduce the heat to medium-low and simmer, covered for about 20-25 minutes.

Step 3

In a large skillet, melt the butter on medium-high heat and sauté the onion, garlic and chile pepper for about 5-7 minutes.

Step 4

Stir in the cooked rice, egg, soy sauce and sesame oil and cook for about 3-5 minutes.

SEAFOOD SAMPLER FRIED RICE

Prep Time: 15 mins - **Total Time:** 55 mins

SERVINGS: 4

NUTRITIONAL VALUE

Calories 304 kcal, Fat 12.2 g, Carbohydrates 37.4g, Protein 11.6 g, Cholesterol 68 mg, Sodium 1294 mg

INGREDIENTS

- 2/3 C. uncooked long grain white rice
- 3 green onions, chopped
- 1 1/3 C. water
- 1 tbsp chopped cilantro
- 3 tbsp vegetable oil
- 1/2 cucumber, sliced
- 2 medium onions, cut into wedges
- 1 lime, sliced
- 3 cloves garlic, chopped
- 1/2 tbsp white sugar
- 2 tsp salt
- 1 egg, beaten
- 1/4 lb. cooked crab meat

DIRECTIONS

Step 1

In a pan, add the rice and water and bring to a boil.

Step 2

Reduce the heat and simmer, covered for about 20 minutes.

Step 3

In a wok, heat the oil on medium heat and sauté the onions and garlic till tender.

Step 4

Stir in the rice, sugar and salt and cook for about 5 minutes.

Step 5

Stir in the egg and increase the heat to high.

Step 6

Stir in the crab meat, green onions and cilantro and cook for about 2-5 minutes.

Step 7

Serve with a garnishing of the cucumber and lime slices.

TERIYAKI FRIED RICE

Prep Time: 10 mins - **Total Time:** 45 mins

SERVINGS: 4

NUTRITIONAL VALUE

Calories 435 kcal, Fat 14.8 g, Carbohydrates 45.9g, Protein 28.3 g, Cholesterol 74 mg, Sodium 1644 mg

INGREDIENTS

- 2 C. water
- 1 (4.5 oz.) can sliced mushrooms, drained
- 1 C. uncooked white rice

- 1/2 C. frozen peas and carrots
- 1 lb. lean ground beef
- 1/2 tsp ground cumin
- 1/4 C. soy sauce, divided
- 3 tbsp teriyaki sauce, divided
- 2 tbsp curry powder, divided

DIRECTIONS

Step 1

In a pan, add the water and rice and bring to a boil.

Step 2

Reduce the heat to medium-low and simmer, covered for about 20-25 minutes.

Step 3

Heat a large skillet on medium-high heat and cook the beef with 1 dash of the soy sauce, 1 tbsp of the teriyaki sauce and 1 tbsp of the curry powder for about 5-7 minutes.

Step 4

Drain the grease from the skillet.

Step 5

Add the mushrooms and frozen vegetables and stir to combine.

Step 6

Reduce the heat to medium-low and cook for about 2 minutes.

Step 7

Fold in the rice.

Step 8

Stir in the remaining soy sauce, teriyaki sauce, curry powder and cumin and cook for about 5 minutes.

CHIVES AND GINGER RAMEN

Prep Time: 1 mins - **Total Time:** 4 mins

SERVINGS: 1

NUTRITIONAL VALUE

Calories 478.3, Fat 18.2g , Cholesterol 186.0mg , Sodium 3816.0mg , Carbohydrates 59.1g , Protein 20.0g

INGREDIENTS

- 1 (3 oz.) packets any flavor ramen
- 1/2 tbsp Sriracha sauce
- noodles (discard the seasoning packet)
- red pepper flakes, to taste
- 1 egg
- 2 tbsp chives
- 1 tbsp freshly grated ginger root
- 1/4 vegetable bouillon cube (cut off a
- small piece)
- 1/4 C. bean sprouts
- 2 -3 tbsp soy sauce

DIRECTIONS

Step 1

In a pan of the boiling water, cook the ramen noodles for about 2 minutes.

Step 2

Add the egg and with a fork immediately stir to combine.

Step 3

Add the ginger, bean sprouts and bullion and cook for about 1 minute.

Step 4

Drain the water.

Step 5

Stir in the soy sauce and Sriracha sauce.

Step 6

Serve with a sprinkling of the red pepper flakes and chives.

HOMEMADE CHINESE HOT AND SOUR

Prep Time: 5 mins - **Total Time:** 15 mins

SERVINGS: 1

NUTRITIONAL VALUE

Calories 466.2, Fat 19.5g , Cholesterol 211.5mg , Sodium 1078.4mg , Carbohydrates 57.6g , Protein 14.7g

INGREDIENTS

- 1 (3 oz.) packages ramen noodles
- 1/8 C. meat, cooked, sliced thinly. (optional) 2 C. water
- 1 green onion, light and dark green parts,
- 1/8 C. mushroom, thinly sliced
- sliced thin

- 1 tbsp rice vinegar
- 1/8 tsp chili sauce
- 1 egg, beaten

DIRECTIONS

Step 1

In a pan, add 2 C. of the warm water, ramen noodles and mushrooms and bring to a boil.

Step 2

Add the rice vinegar and chili cSauce and cook for about 5-7 minutes.

Step 3

Reduce the heat to medium.

Step 4

Add the sliced meat and stir to combine.

Step 5

Very slowly drizzle, add the beaten egg, stirring continuously.

Step 6

Divide the soup into serving bowls and serve hot with a sprinkling of the sliced onion.

RED CHILE RAMEN AND DUCK

Prep Time: 10 mins - **Total Time:** 45 mins

SERVINGS: 4

NUTRITIONAL VALUE

Calories 282.7, Fat 9.4g , Cholesterol 7.2mg , Sodium 789.1mg , Carbohydrates 39.4g , Protein 10.5g

INGREDIENTS

- 5 C. water
- 150 g dried ramen noodles
- 4 C. chicken stock
- bean sprouts, to garnish
- 2 red chilies, seeded and halved
- red Chile, to garnish
- 8 slices ginger
- coriander, to garnish (cilentro)
- 3 tbsp lemon juice
- 3 bunches bok choy (optional)
- 3 stalks lemongrass, bruised
- salt
- 2 sprigs coriander
- white pepper
- 1 Chinese barbecued duck, deboned and
- chopped
- 4 shallots, chopped

DIRECTIONS

Step 1

In a pan, add the stock and water and heat till liquid is simmering.

Step 2

Add, galangal, chillies, lime juice, lemon grass stalks and coriander and simmer for about 20 minutes.

Step 3

Through a strainer, strain the liquid and return to pan.

Step 4

Add the duck and shallots and bring to a boil.

Step 5

Meanwhile in another pan of the salted boiling water, cook the ramen noodles ; cook ,for about 3-5 minutes.

Step 6

Drain the noodles

Step 7

Add noodles and bok choy into soup stock and simmer for about 5 minutes.

Step 8

Stir in salt and pepper and remove from the heat.

Step 9

Divide soup into serving bowls and serve hot with a garnishing of the bean sprouts, chili strips and coriander.

JAPANESE EGGS FOR RAMEN

Prep Time: 30 mins - **Total Time:** 12 hrs 30 mins

SERVINGS: 2

NUTRITIONAL VALUE

Calories 268.4, Fat 7.1g , Cholesterol 279.0mg , Sodium 292.4mg , Carbohydrates 28.9g , Protein 9.6g

INGREDIENTS

- 1/2 C. water
- 1/4 C. sugar

- 1/2 C. rice cooking wine
- 3 eggs
- 1/4 C. mirin
- 1/4 soy sauce

DIRECTIONS

Step 1

In a bowl, add the water, mirin, rice wine, soy sauce, and sugar and beat till sugar is dissolved.

Step 2

In a medium pan, add 1 quart of the water on high heat and bring to a boil.

Step 3

Carefully, place the eggs into water.

Step 4

Reduce the heat and cook for about 7 1/2 minutes.

Step 5

Drain the eggs and transfer into a bowl of the ice water.

Step 6

Cool for 3 minutes and then carefully, peel the eggs.

Step 7

Transfer the eggs into a bowl and cover the sauce mixture.

Step 8

Place a double layer of paper towels on top and press down to keep eggs submerged and marinating evenly.

Step 9

Refrigerate, covered for at least 4 hours or up to

Step 12

Step10

Discard the marinade ad serve alongside the noodles.

Step 11

You can store the eggs in refrigerator by placing in a sealed container for up to 3 days.

BEEF SATAY DINNER

Prep Time: 30 mins - **Total Time:** 38 mins

SERVINGS: 4

NUTRITIONAL VALUE

Calories 794.6, Fat 43.3g , Cholesterol 154.2mg , Sodium 1959.2mg , Carbohydrates 39.6g , Protein 63.0g

INGREDIENTS

DIRECTIONS

- FOR MARINADE

Step 1

Set your grill for medium-high heat and

- 2 tbsp soy sauce
- lightly, grease the grill grate.
- 2 tbsp lime juice

Step 2

Soak 12 wooden skewers in the water for

- 1 1/2 tsp sugar

- about 15 minutes.
- 1 1/2 tsp fresh ginger, grated, peeled

Step 3

In a shallow dish, mix together 2 tbsp of 1 garlic clove, grated (optional)

- each soy sauce and lime juice and 1 1/2
- 1/4 tsp red pepper flakes (optional)
- tsp of each sugar and ginger and 1/4 tsp
- 2 lb. flank steaks, thinly sliced against the of the red pepper flakes.
- grain

Step 4

Add the beef and toss to coat. Keep aside FOR PEANUT SAUCE

- for about 10 minutes.
- 1 tbsp lime juice

Step 5

Meanwhile, in a blender, add the remaining 1 tsp sugar

- 1 tbsp of the lime juice, 1 tsp of the sugar, 1 tsp fresh ginger, grated and peeled
- 1 tsp of the ginger, peanut butter, 1/3 C. of 1/3 C. creamy peanut butter
- the water and soy sauce and pulse till well
- 1/3 C. water
- combined.
- 1 tbsp soy sauce

Step 6

Transfer the mixture into a bowl with the 1/4 tsp red pepper flakes (optional)

- chopped peanuts, green onions and 1/4
- FOR RAMEN
- tsp of the red pepper flakes and stir to
- 1/4 C. roasted peanuts, chopped
- combine.
- 3 green onions, sliced
- vegetable oil, for grill

Step 7

Add the ramen noodles and toss to coat.

- 2 (3 oz.) packages ramen noodles, cooked

Step 8

Thread the beef onto skewers and cook on

- according to package instructions (
- grill for about 3-4 minutes per side.
- seasoning packet discarded)

Step 9

Serve the beef skewers with the ramen

BOK CHOY STIR FRY

Prep Time: 15 mins - **Total Time:** 20 mins

SERVINGS: 3

NUTRITIONAL VALUE

Calories 90 kcal, Fat 6.9 g, Carbohydrates 5.9g, Protein 2.2 g, Cholesterol 0 mg, Sodium 358 mg

INGREDIENTS

- 3 small heads bok choy, chopped
- 1/2 tsp red pepper flakes (optional)
- 1 tbsp vegetable oil
- 1 tbsp soy sauce
- 1 red bell pepper, sliced
- 6 drops toasted sesame oil
- 2 cloves garlic, chopped
- 1 tbsp grated fresh ginger

DIRECTIONS

Step 1

Trim the bottom of boy choy heads and cut the leaves from the stalks.

Step 2

Cut the stalks into 1/2-inch pieces.

Step 3

Cut the large leaves into halves

Step 4

In a large skillet, heat the vegetable oil on high heat and sauté the Bok choy stalks and bell pepper for about 1 minute.

Step 5

Stir in the garlic, ginger and red pepper flakes and sauté for about 1 minute.

Step 6

Stir in the bok choy leaves, soy sauce and sesame oil and sauté for about 1 minute more.

CHINESE TURKEY EGG ROLLS

Prep Time: 45 mins - **Total Time:** 1 hr 5 mins

SERVINGS: 20

NUTRITIONAL VALUE

Calories 206 kcal, Fat 10.8 g, Carbohydrates 21.1g, Protein 6 g, Cholesterol 12 mg, Sodium 248 mg

INGREDIENTS

- 2 quarts oil for deep frying
- 3/4 C. shredded carrots
- 1/2 lb. ground turkey
- 2 green onions, finely chopped
- 2 tbsp chopped fresh ginger root
- 1 tsp soy sauce
- 3 cloves garlic, peeled and minced
- 2 (12 oz.) packages wonton wrappers
- 2 tsp sesame oil
- 1 medium head bok choy, shredded

DIRECTIONS

Step 1

In a large, heavy pan, heat the oil to 375 degrees F.

Step 2

In a large, deep skillet, add the ground turkey, 1/2 of the ginger root and 1/2 of the garlic on high heat and cook till browned completely.

Step 3

In another skillet, heat the sesame oil on medium-high heat and sauté the remaining ginger and garlic till aromatic.

Step 4

Add the bok choy, carrots, green onions and soy sauce and cook till the vegetables are tender but crisp.

Step 5

Remove from the heat.

Step 6

In a medium bowl, mix together the turkey and Bok choy mixture.

Step 7

Fill a double thickness of the wonton wrappers with 1 tbsp of the turkey and bok choy mixture.

Step 8

Fold the wrappers over the filling and moisten seam to seal.

Step 9

Repeat with remaining wrappers and filling.

Step10

Fry the filled in batches for about 3-5 minutes.

NORTH CHINESE STYLE CABBAGE

Prep Time: 15 mins - **Total Time:** 22 mins

SERVINGS: 2

NUTRITIONAL VALUE

Calories 317 kcal, Fat 27.5 g, Carbohydrates 17.9g, Protein 1.8 g, Cholesterol 0 mg, Sodium 270 mg

INGREDIENTS

- 1 1/2 tbsp white sugar
- 1/2 lb. baby bok choy, trimmed and
- 1 tbsp brown rice vinegar
- chopped
- 1 1/2 tbsp cornstarch
- salt to taste
- 3 tbsp cold water
- 1/4 C. vegetable oil
- 3 dried red chili peppers, seeded and
- thinly sliced

DIRECTIONS

Step 1

In a bowl, mix together the sugar, brown rice vinegar, cornstarch and cold water.

Step 2

In a large skillet, heat the oil on high heat and sauté the chili peppers for about 4 minutes.

Step 3

With a slotted spoon, transfer the chili peppers into a bowl.

Step 4

Add the bok choy and cook for about 1-2 minutes.

Step 5

Add the vinegar sauce and bring to a boil.

Step 6

Cook for about 30 seconds.

Step 7

Remove from the heat and season with the salt.

HANOI STYLE CHICKEN PHO

Prep Time: 10 mins - **Total Time:** 40 mins

SERVINGS: 2

NUTRITIONAL VALUE

Calories 521 kcal, Fat 13.7 g, Carbohydrates 54.4g, Protein 49.8 g, Cholesterol 107 mg, Sodium 3270 mg

INGREDIENTS

- 4 oz. dry Chinese egg noodles
- 5 green onions, chopped
- 6 C. chicken stock
- 2 C. cubed cooked chicken
- 2 tbsp fish sauce
- 1 C. bean sprouts
- 4 cloves garlic, minced
- 1 C. chopped bok choy
- 2 tsp minced fresh ginger root
- 1 tbsp minced lemon grass

DIRECTIONS

Step 1

In large pan of the boiling water, cook the noodles for about 8 minutes.

Step 2

Drain well.

Step 3

In a large pan, add the chicken stock, fish sauce, garlic, ginger, lemon grass and green onions and bring to a boil.

Step 4

Reduce the heat and simmer for about 10 minutes.

Step 5

Stir in the chicken, bean sprouts and bok choy and simmer for about 5 minutes.

Step 6

Divide the cooked noodles between 2 large bowls and top with the pho.

Step 7

Serve immediately.

CREAM CHEESE WONTONS

Prep Time: 15 mins - **Total Time:** 25 mins

SERVINGS: 2

NUTRITIONAL VALUE

Calories 312 kcal, Fat 19 g, Carbohydrates 25.6g, Protein 10.4 g, Cholesterol 43 mg, Sodium 491 mg

INGREDIENTS

- 1 quart oil for frying
- 1 (8 oz.) package cream cheese, softened
- 1 tbsp vegetable oil
- 1 tbsp soy sauce
- 1 clove garlic, minced

- 1 (14 oz.) package small won ton
- 2 tbsp minced onion
- wrappers
- 1 medium head bok choy, chopped
- 2 tbsp chopped snow peas
- 1 (6 oz.) can crab meat, drained

DIRECTIONS

Step 1

In a deep-fryer, heat the oil to 375 degrees F.

Step 2

In a large skillet, heat 1 tbsp of the vegetable oil and sauté the garlic and onion for about 2 minutes.

Step 3

Add the bok choy and pea pods and stir fry till the bok choy and pea pods are crisp-tender.

Step 4

In a large bowl, mix together the crab, cream cheese, soy sauce and sautéed vegetable mixture.

Step 5

Place 3/4 tsp of the mixture into the center of each won ton wrapper.

Step 6

Fold the wrappers in half to make a triangle and with wet fingers, seal the wrapper around the mixture, pressing the ends together.

Step 7

Fry the dumplings in the prepared oil in batches till golden brown.

Step 8

Transfer the dumplings onto paper towel lined plates to drain 74

NATIONAL PHILIPPINES FISH STEW

Prep Time: 5 mins - **Total Time:** 15 mins

SERVINGS: 4

NUTRITIONAL VALUE

Calories 112 kcal, Fat 1 g, Carbohydrates 13.4g, Protein 13.1 g, Cholesterol 21 mg, Sodium 63 mg

INGREDIENTS

- 1/2 lb. tilapia fillets, cut into chunks
- 3 C. water
- 1 small head bok choy, chopped
- 2 dried red chili peppers (optional)
- 2 medium tomatoes, cut into chunks
- 1 C. thinly sliced daikon radish
- 1/4 C. tamarind paste

DIRECTIONS

Step 1

In a medium pan, mix together the tilapia, bok choy, tomatoes and radish.

Step 2

In a bowl, mix together the tamarind paste and water.

Step 3

Add the tamarind paste into the pan with the chili peppers and bring to a boil.

Step 4

Cook for about 5 minutes.

Step 5

Serve hot

TAISHAN CHOW MEIN

Prep Time: 20 mins - **Total Time:** 55 mins

SERVINGS: 4

NUTRITIONAL VALUE

Calories 526 kcal, Fat 17.9 g, Carbohydrates 61.7g, Protein 29.4 g, Cholesterol 30 mg, Sodium 992 mg

INGREDIENTS

- 2 tsp soy sauce
- 1 tsp minced garlic
- 1 tsp cornstarch
- 2 heads bok choy, chopped
- 1/4 tsp sesame oil
- 1/2 zucchini, diced
- 1/2 lb. skinless, boneless chicken breast
- 10 sugar snap peas
- halves, cut into strips
- 1 carrot, cut into thin strips
- 3/4 C. chicken broth
- 2 tbsp chopped green onion
- 2 tbsp oyster sauce

- 3/4 tsp white sugar
- 1/2 lb. chow mein noodles
- 1 tbsp vegetable oil

DIRECTIONS

Step 1

In a large bowl, add the soy sauce, corn starch and sesame oil and beat till smooth.

Step 2

Add the chicken strips and toss to coat. Refrigerate, covered for at least 20 minutes.

Step 3

In another bowl, mix together the chicken broth, oyster sauce and sugar and keep aside.

Step 4

In a large pan of lightly salted boiling water, cook the noodles for about 4-5 minutes.

Step 5

Drain well and keep aside. Drain and rinse under cold water.

Step 6

In a large skillet, heat the vegetable oil and sauté the garlic for about 30 seconds.

Step 7

Add the marinated chicken and cook for about 5-6 minutes.

Step 8

Transfer the chicken mixture into a plate.

Step 9

In the same skillet, add the bok choy, zucchini, snap peas and carrot and cook for about 2 minutes.

Step10

Add the noodles, chicken mixture and broth mixture and cook for about 2 minutes.

Step 11

Serve with a garnishing of the green onions.

MALAYSIAN ENTREE MEAL

Prep Time: 15 mins - **Total Time:** 50 mins

SERVINGS: 2

NUTRITIONAL VALUE

Calories 658 kcal, Fat 16.3 g, Carbohydrates 82.1g, Protein 42.1 g, Cholesterol 255 mg, Sodium 1555 mg

INGREDIENTS

- 1 C. uncooked white rice
- 2 tbsp light soy sauce
- 2 C. water
- 1 tbsp yeast extract spread (such as
- 1/2 lb. ground chicken
- Marmite(R))
- 1/2 tbsp light-colored soy sauce
- white pepper to taste
- ground white pepper
- 1 tbsp vegetable oil
- 1 clove garlic, minced
- 2 bok choy stalks, chopped
- 2 eggs, lightly beaten

DIRECTIONS

Step 1

In a pan, add the rice and water and bring to a boil on high heat.

Step 2

Reduce the heat to medium-low and simmer, covered for about 20-25 minutes.

Step 3

Remove from the heat and keep aside to cool completely.

Step 4

In a bowl, mix together the chicken, 1/2 tbsp of the soy sauce and pepper.

Step 5

In a skillet, heat 1 tbsp of the oil on high heat and cook the garlic and chicken till browned, breaking the chicken into bits.

Step 6

Add the bok choy, cooled rice and pepper and stir fry for about 1 minute.

Step 7

Reduce the heat to medium and make a hole in the middle of the chicken mixture.

Step 8

Carefully, place the beaten eggs into the hole and cook for about 1 minute.

Step 9

Cover the top of the eggs with the rice and cook for about 30 seconds.

Step10

Stir in 2 tbsp soy sauce.

Step 11

Stir in the yeast extract spread and cook till slightly brownish in color.

Step 12

Stir in some pepper and serve.

PHILIPPINES SOUP

Prep Time: 30 mins - **Total Time:** 55 mins

SERVINGS: 4

NUTRITIONAL VALUE

Calories 532 kcal, Fat 22.9 g, Carbohydrates 14.1g, Protein 65.5 g, Cholesterol 208 mg, Sodium 1512 mg

INGREDIENTS

- 1 tbsp cooking oil
- bite-sized pieces
- 1 onion, chopped
- salt and pepper to taste
- 2 cloves garlic, minced
- 1 head bok choy, chopped
- 1 (1 1/2 inch) piece fresh ginger, peeled
- 1/2 lb. spinach
- and thinly sliced
- 1 tbsp fish sauce
- 3 lb. chicken legs and thighs, rinsed and
- patted dry
- 2 (14 oz.) cans chicken broth
- 1 chayote squash, peeled and cut into

DIRECTIONS

Step 1

In a large pan, heat the oil on medium heat and sauté the onion and garlic till fragrant.

Step 2

Stir in the ginger and fish sauce.

Step 3

Add the chicken and cook for about 5 minutes.

Step 4

Add the chicken broth and cook for about 5 minutes.

Step 5

Add the chayote and simmer for about 10 minutes.

Step 6

Add the salt, pepper, bok choy and spinach and cook for about 1-2 minutes.

Step 7

Serve hot.

VEGGIE CURRY CARIBBEAN STYLE

Prep Time: 20 mins - **Total Time:** 50 mins

SERVINGS: 6

NUTRITIONAL VALUE

Calories 190 kcal, Fat 9.4 g, Carbohydrates 25.8g, Protein 2.7 g, Cholesterol 0 mg, Sodium 19 mg

INGREDIENTS

- 1 tsp ground cumin

- 1/2 C. chopped red bell pepper
- 1/2 tsp ground turmeric
- 1/2 C. chopped broccoli
- 1/2 tsp curry powder
- 1 C. chopped bok choy
- 1/2 tsp ground allspice
- 1 plantains, peeled and broken into chunks
- 1/4 C. olive oil
- 1 C. water
- 1 tbsp grated fresh ginger root
- salt to taste
- 1 small onion, chopped
- 4 cloves garlic, minced
- 2 potatoes, cut into small cubes

DIRECTIONS

Step 1

In a small bowl, mix together the cumin, turmeric, allspice and curry powder.

Step 2

In a skillet, heat the olive oil on medium-low heat and sauté the ginger and cumin mixture for about 5 minutes.

Step 3

Add the onion and garlic and sauté for about 1-2 minutes.

Step 4

Stir in the potatoes and cook for about 1-2 minutes.

Step 5

Add the red bell pepper, broccoli, bok choy, plantains and enough water to reach about half-full and simmer, covered for about 20-25 minutes.

Step 6

Season with the salt and serve.

PAMPANGA OXTAIL STEW

Prep Time: 20 mins - **Total Time:** 2 hrs 50 mins

SERVINGS: 6

NUTRITIONAL VALUE

Calories 1062 kcal, Fat 54.9 g, Carbohydrates 28.1g, Protein 116.1 g, Cholesterol 375 mg, Sodium 1010 mg

INGREDIENTS

- 4 1/2 lb. beef oxtails
- 1 onion, chopped
- 3 C. water
- 2 cloves garlic, minced
- 2 beef bouillon cubes
- 1 tsp achiote powder
- 1/2 lb. bok choy, chopped
- 3 tbsp smooth peanut butter
- 1/2 lb. long beans, cut into bite-sized
- pieces
- 1/2 lb. eggplant, cubed

- 2 tbsp olive oil

DIRECTIONS

Step 1

In a large pan, add the oxtails and water and bring to a boil.

Step 2

Reduce the heat to medium-low and simmer for about 2 hours, removing the fat from the top of the liquid as possible.

Step 3

Crumble the beef bouillon cubes into the pan and stir to dissolve.

Step 4

Transfer the meat into a plate and keep aside.

Step 5

In the pan, add the bok choy, long beans and eggplant and simmer till tender.

Step 6

Meanwhile in another large pan, heat the olive oil on medium heat and sauté the onion and garlic till tender.

Step 7

Add the achiote powder and peanut butter and stir till melted completely.

Step 8

Add about half the broth and bring to a boil for about 5 minutes.

Step 9

Add the oxtails and cook for about 5 minutes.

Step10

Add the remaining broth with the vegetables and serve hot..

FILIPIN FILLING SOUP

Prep Time: 15 mins - **Total Time:** 1 hr

SERVINGS: 6

NUTRITIONAL VALUE

Calories 304 kcal, Fat 19.7 g, Carbohydrates 15g, Protein 17.8 g, Cholesterol 51 mg, Sodium 1405 mg

INGREDIENTS

- 2 tbsp canola oil
- 1/2 medium head bok choy, cut into 1 1/2
- 1 large onion, chopped
- inch strips
- 2 cloves garlic, chopped
- 1 head fresh broccoli, cut into bite size pieces 1 lb. beef stew meat, cut into 1 inch cubes
- 1 (1.41 oz.) package tamarind soup base
- 1 quart water
- 2 large tomatoes, diced
- 1/2 lb. fresh green beans, rinsed and
- trimmed

DIRECTIONS

Step 1

In a pan, heat the oil and sauté the onion and garlic till tender.

Step 2

Add the beef and seat till browned completely.

Step 3

Add the water and bring to a boil.

Step 4

Reduce the heat and simmer for about 20-30 minutes.

Step 5

Add the tomatoes and green beans and simmer for about 10 minutes.

Step 6

Stir in the bok choy, broccoli and tamarind soup mix and simmer for an about 10

RISING SUN SALAD

Prep Time: 25 mins - **Total Time:** 25 mins

SERVINGS: 4

NUTRITIONAL VALUE

Calories 361 kcal, Fat 34.4 g, Carbohydrates 10.1g, Protein 4.6 g, Cholesterol 0 mg, Sodium 764 mg

INGREDIENTS

- 1/2 C. canola oil
- 1 carrot, cut into matchsticks
- 1/4 C. rice vinegar
- 1/4 C. toasted sliced almonds
- 3 tbsp soy sauce
- 1/2 C. croutons
- 1 tbsp mirin (Japanese sweet rice wine)
- 2 tbsp toasted sesame seeds

- 1/2 head romaine lettuce, chopped
- 2 heads baby bok choy, cleaned and
- sliced

DIRECTIONS

Step 1

In a small bowl, add the oil, vinegar, soy sauce, mirin and sesame seeds and beat till well combined.

Step 2

In a large bowl, mix together the romaine, Bok choy, carrot, almonds, and croutons.

Step 3

Place the dressing over the salad and toss to coat.

Step 4

Serve immediately.

BABY MUSHROOM BAKE

Prep Time: 10 mins - **Total Time:** 40 mins

SERVINGS: 8

NUTRITIONAL VALUE

Calories 163 kcal, Fat 3.8 g, Carbohydrates 26.5g, Protein 3.9 g, Cholesterol 2 mg, Sodium < 389 mg

INGREDIENTS

- 2 tbsp extra-virgin olive oil
- 1/4 C. dry white wine
- 1 C. chopped leeks

- 3 C. Swanson(R) Chicken Broth
- 6 oz. baby Bella (Crimini) or white
- 3 C. chopped bok choy
- mushrooms, sliced
- 1 1/4 C. uncooked long grain white rice

DIRECTIONS

Step 1

Set your oven to 400 degrees F before doing anything else.

Step 2

In a large oven-proof skillet, heat the oil on medium-high heat and sauté the leeks for about 3 minutes.

Step 3

Add the mushrooms and cook for about 3-5 minutes.

Step 4

Add the rice and cook, stirring till the rice is coated with oil completely.

Step 5

Add the wine and bring to a gentle boil on medium heat.

Step 6

Cook for about 1 minute.

Step 7

Add the chicken broth and bring to a boil.

Step 8

Cover the skillet and immediately, place in the oven.

Step 9

Cook in the oven for about 10 minutes.

Step10

Gently stir in bok choy and cook for about 10 minutes.

Step 11

Remove from the oven and stir.

Step 12

Keep aside, covered for about 10 minutes before serving.

HOLIDAY DUCK ROAST

Prep Time: 45 mins - **Total Time:** 1 hr 30 mins

SERVINGS: 4

NUTRITIONAL VALUE

Calories 846 kcal, Fat 32.9 g, Carbohydrates 111.7g, Protein 33.2 g, Cholesterol 121 mg, Sodium 1589 mg

INGREDIENTS

- 2 tsp salt
- 3 slices pancetta, cut into thin strips
- 1 tsp fresh-ground black pepper
- 6 shallots, thinly sliced
- 1 1/2 tbsp dried thyme leaves
- 1/2 C. sliced shiitake mushrooms
- 1 tbsp crushed dried rosemary
- 2 lb. bok choy, sliced
- 3 tbsp olive oil

- 4 (8 oz.) boneless duck breast halves
- 4 potatoes, cubed
- 2 tbsp vegetable oil
- 2 pints fresh blueberries
- 1 tbsp butter
- 1/2 C. water
- 2 tbsp aged balsamic vinegar
- 1/2 C. apple juice
- 1/2 C. white sugar
- 1 jalapeno pepper, finely chopped

DIRECTIONS

Step 1

Set your oven to 375 degrees F before doing anything else.

Step 2

In a small bowl mix together the salt, ground black pepper, thyme and rosemary.

Step 3

In a 13x9-inch baking dish, place the cubed potatoes, olive oil and 2 tbsp of the herb mixture and toss to coat well.

Step 4

Spread the potato cubes in a single layer in the baking dish.

Step 5

Cook in the oven for about 35-40 minutes.

Step 6

Meanwhile in a small pan, mix together the blueberries, water, apple juice, sugar and jalapeño on medium-high heat and bring to a boil.

Step 7

Reduce the heat to low and simmer for about 10 minutes.

Step 8

Heat a large skillet on medium heat and cook the pancetta ill crispy.

Step 9

Transfer the pancetta onto a paper towel lined plate to drain, leaving the drippings in the skillet. Holiday Duck Roast

Step10

In the same skillet, add the shallots and mushrooms and cook till soft and just beginning to brown.

Step 11

Transfer the shallots and mushrooms into a plate and keep aside.

Step 12

Increase heat to medium-high and stir fry the bok choy for about 5 minutes.

Step 13

Stir in the shallots, mushrooms and pancetta and remove from the heat.

Step 14

Rinse the duck breast halves and pat dry.

Step 15

Rub the remaining herb mixture over the duck breasts evenly.

Step 16

Heat a large skillet on medium-high heat and add the vegetable oil and butter.

Step 17

Immediately place the duck breasts, skin and fat side down and cook for about 5 minutes, without stirring.

Step 18

Flip the breasts and cook till cooked completely.

Step 19

Transfer the duck into a plate and cover with a piece of the foil for about 5 minutes.

Step 20

Now, place the skillet with the bok choy mixture on medium heat and cook till warmed completely.

Step 21

Cut each duck breast into 1/2-inch strips diagonally.

Step 22

Divide the bok choy mixture in serving plates and drizzle with the aged balsamic vinegar evenly.

Step 23

Top with the duck breasts slices, followed by the blueberry sauce.

Step 24

Serve alongside the roasted potatoes.

THURSDAYS GINGER CHINESE CELLOPHANE NOODLES

Prep Time: 25 mins - **Total Time:** 45 mins

SERVINGS: 4

NUTRITIONAL VALUE

Calories 360 kcal, Fat 9.6 g, Carbohydrates 62.2g, Protein 10.6 g, Cholesterol 0 mg, Sodium 1639 mg

INGREDIENTS

- 2 tbsp coconut oil
- 12 C. vegetable broth
- 2 1/2 lb. bok choy, cut into bite-sized
- 2 (2 oz.) packages cellophane noodles
- pieces
- 3 C. fresh bean sprouts
- 6 cloves garlic, grated
- 5 scallions, trimmed and thinly sliced
- 1 (3 inch) piece fresh ginger, grated
- 3 C. shredded carrots
- 2 tsp Chinese five-spice powder
- 1 tsp ground cumin

DIRECTIONS

Step 1

In a large pan, melt the coconut oil on medium-high heat and stir fry the bok choy for about 3-5 minutes.

Step 2

Stir in the garlic and ginger and stir fry for about 1 minute.

Step 3

Add the carrots, five-spice powder, cumin and vegetable broth and bring to a boil.

Step 4

Add the noodles and reduce the heat and simmer for about 3 minutes.

Step 5

Stir in the bean sprouts and scallions and remove from the heat.

Step 6

Keep aside for about 5 minutes before serving.

CRAB RANGOON

Prep Time: 15 mins **- Total Time:** 25 mins

SERVINGS: 10

NUTRITIONAL VALUE

Calories 312 kcal, Fat 19 g, Carbohydrates 25.6g, Protein 10.4 g, Cholesterol 43 mg, Sodium 491 mg

INGREDIENTS

- 1 quart oil for frying
- 1 (8 oz.) package cream cheese, softened
- 1 tbsp vegetable oil
- 1 tbsp soy sauce
- 1 clove garlic, minced
- 1 (14 oz.) package small won ton wrappers
- 2 tbsps minced onion
- 1 medium head bok choy, diced
- 2 tbsps diced snow peas
- 1 (6 oz.) can crab meat, drained

DIRECTIONS

Step 1

Get a large pot or Dutch oven and get your oil hot to 375 degrees before doing anything else.

Step 2

Now being to stir fry your onions and garlic for 3 mins then combine in the pea pods and bok choy.

Step 3

Fry the veggies until they are crisp for a few mins.

Step 4

Now get a bowl, mix: stir fry veggies, crab, soy sauce, and cream cheese.

Step 5

Place a tsp of mix into the middle of your wonton wrapper and from the wrapper into a triangle. Use a bit of water and some pinching to seal the edges.

Step 6

Fry your ragoon in the oil until browned.

Step 7

Enjoy..

CLASSICAL PAD THAI NOODLES I

Prep Time: 30 mins - **Total Time:** 2 hrs

SERVINGS: 4

NUTRITIONAL VALUE

Calories 397 kcal, Carbohydrates 39.5 g, Cholesterol 41 mg, Fat 23.3 g, Protein 13.2 g, Sodium 1234 mg

INGREDIENTS

- 2/3 cup dried rice vermicelli
- 3 tbsps chopped peanuts
- 1/4 cup peanut oil

- 1 pound bean sprouts, divided
- 2/3 cup thinly sliced firm tofu
- 3 green onions, whites cut thinly across
- 1 large egg, beaten
- and greens sliced into thin lengths -
- 4 cloves garlic, finely chopped
- divided
- 1/4 cup vegetable broth
- 3 tbsps chopped peanuts
- 2 tbsps fresh lime juice
- 2 limes, cut into wedges for garnish
- 2 tbsps soy sauce
- 1 tbsp white sugar
- 1 tsp salt
- 1/2 tsp dried red chili flakes

DIRECTIONS

Step 1

Put rice vermicelli noodles in hot water for about 30 minutes before draining the water.

Step 2

Cook tofu in hot oil until golden brown before draining it with paper tower.

Step 3

Reserve 1 tbsp of oil for later use and cook egg in the remaining hot oil until done, and set them aside for later use.

Step 4

Now cook noodles and garlic in the hot reserved oil, while coating them well with this oil along the way.

Step 5

In this pan containing noodles; add tofu, salt, chili flakes, egg and 3 tbsps peanuts, and mix all this very thoroughly.

Step 6

Also add bean sprouts and green onion into it, while reserving some for the garnishing purposes. Cook all this for two minutes before transferring to a serving platter.

Step 7

Garnish this with peanuts and the reserved vegetables before placing some lime wedges around the platter to make this dish more attractive.

Step 8

CLASSICAL PAD THAI NOODLES II

Prep Time: 15 mins - **Total Time:** 25 mins

SERVINGS: 4

NUTRITIONAL VALUE

Calories 352 kcal, Carbohydrates 46.8 g, Cholesterol 46 mg, Fat 15 g, Protein 9.2 g, Sodium 335 mg

INGREDIENTS

- 1 (6.75 ounce) package thin rice noodles
- 2 tbsps chopped peanuts
- 2 tbsps vegetable oil
- 1 cup fresh bean sprouts
- 3 ounces fried tofu, sliced into thin strips
- 1 tbsp chopped fresh cilantro

- 1 clove garlic, minced
- 1 lime, cut into wedges
- 1 egg
- 1 tbsp soy sauce
- 1 pinch white sugar

DIRECTIONS

Step 1

In a heatproof bowl containing noodles, pour boiling water and let it stand as it is for about five minutes before draining the water and setting it aside for later use.

Step 2

Fry garlic in hot oil until brown before adding noodles frying it for about one minute.

Step 3

Now add egg into it and break it up when it starts to get solid, and mix it well into the noodles.

Step 4

Now add soy sauce, tofu, cilantro, bean sprouts, sugar and peanuts into it and mix it well.

Step 5

Remove from heat and add lime wedges just before you serve..

SUPER EASY COCONUT SOUP THAI-STYLE

Prep Time: 15 mins **- Total Time:** 40 mins

SERVINGS: 8

NUTRITIONAL VALUE

Calories 314 kcal, Carbohydrates 17.2 g, Cholesterol 86 mg, Fat 21.6 g, Protein 15.3 g, Sodium 523 mg

INGREDIENTS

- 1 pound medium shrimp - peeled and
- 3 tbsps fish sauce
- deveined
- 1/4 cup brown sugar
- 2 (13.5 ounce) cans canned coconut
- 1 tsp curry powder
- milk
- 1 tbsp green onion, thinly sliced
- 2 cups water
- 1 tsp dried red pepper flakes
- 1 (1 inch) piece galangal, thinly sliced
- 4 stalks lemon grass, bruised and
- chopped
- 10 kaffir lime leaves, torn in half
- 1 pound shiitake mushrooms, sliced
- 1/4 cup lime juice

DIRECTIONS

Step 1

Cook shrimp in boiling water until tender.

Step 2

Put coconut milk, water, lime leaves, galangal and lemon grass in a large sized pan and heat it up for about 10 minutes before transferring the coconut milk into a new pan, while discarding all the spices.

Step 3

Heat up shiitake mushrooms in the coconut milk for five minutes before adding lime juice, curry powder, brown sugar and fish sauce into it.

Step 4

When you want to serve it, heat up the shrimp in this soup for some time before pouring this into serving bowls.

CURRY THAI INSPIRED CHICKEN WITH PINEAPPLE

Prep Time: 15 mins - **Total Time:** 50 mins

SERVINGS: 6

NUTRITIONAL VALUE

Calories 623 kcal, Carbohydrates 77.5 g, Cholesterol 20 mg, Fat 34.5 g, Protein 20.3 g, Sodium 781 mg

INGREDIENTS

- 2 cups uncooked jasmine rice
- 1/2 red bell pepper, julienned
- 1 quart water
- 1/2 green bell pepper, julienned
- 1/4 cup red curry paste
- 1/2 small onion, chopped
- 2 (13.5 ounce) cans coconut milk
- 1 cup pineapple chunks, drained

- 2 skinless, boneless chicken breast halves
- - cut into thin strips
- 3 tbsps fish sauce
- 1/4 cup white sugar
- 1 1/2 cups sliced bamboo shoots, drained

DIRECTIONS

Step 1

Bring the mixture of rice and water to boil before turning the heat down to low and cooking for 25 minutes.

Step 2

Add coconut milk, bamboo shoots, chicken, sugar and fish sauce to the mixture of curry paste and 1 can coconut milk in a pan before bringing all this to boil and cooking for 15 minutes.

Step 3

Into this mixture, add red bell pepper, onion and green bell pepper, and cook all this for ten more minutes or until you see that the peppers are tender.

Step 4

Add pineapple after removing from heat and serve this on top of cooked rice.

SIMPLE AND EASY CLASSICAL PEANUT SAUCE

Prep Time: 10 mins - **Total Time:** 10 mins

SERVINGS: 6

NUTRITIONAL VALUE

Calories 130 kcal, Carbohydrates 9.8 g, Cholesterol 3 mg, Fat 9.5 g, Protein 2.7 g, Sodium 529 mg

INGREDIENTS

- 1/4 cup creamy peanut butter
- 1/4 cup soy sauce
- 3 cloves garlic, minced
- 2 tbsps fresh lemon juice
- 1/4 cup brown sugar
- 1/4 cup mayonnaise

DIRECTIONS

Step 1

Whisk all the ingredients that are mentioned above in a medium sized bowl and refrigerate it for at least two hours before you serve it to anyone.

THE BEST ORANGE THAI CHICKEN

Prep Time: 15 mins - **Total Time:** 40 mins

SERVINGS: 12

NUTRITIONAL VALUE

Calories 427 kcal, Carbohydrates 37.1 g, Cholesterol 32 mg, Fat 24.3 g, Protein 18.4 g, Sodium 1360 mg

INGREDIENTS

- 2 tbsps olive oil
- 1/3 cup orange juice
- 3 carrots, cut into matchsticks
- 1/3 cup soy sauce
- 1/2 tsp minced fresh ginger root

- 1/3 cup brown sugar
- 1 clove garlic, minced
- 2 tbsps ketchup
- 2 tbsps olive oil
- 1 tsp crushed red pepper flakes
- 2 skinless, boneless chicken breast halves,
- 2 tbsps cornstarch
- cut into small pieces
- 1/2 cup water
- 1/2 cup peanuts

DIRECTIONS

Step 1

Cook carrots, garlic and ginger in hot olive oil for about 5 minutes before transferring it to a bowl.

Step 2

Cook chicken in hot olive oil for about 10 minutes before adding carrot mixture, water, brown sugar , orange juice, soy sauce, peanuts, ketchup, and red pepper flakes into this, and cooking for another 5 minutes.

Step 3

Take out ¼ cup of sauce from the pan and add cornstarch into it.

Step 4

Add this cornstarch mixture back to the chicken and cook until you see that the required thickness has been reached.

SPICY THAI PASTA

Prep Time: 15 mins - **Total Time:** 20 mins

SERVINGS: 8

NUTRITIONAL VALUE

Calories 564 kcal, Carbohydrates 52.4 g, Cholesterol 230 mg, Fat 19.3 g, Protein 46.3 g, Sodium 375 mg

INGREDIENTS

- 1 (12 ounce) package rice vermicelli
- 1 1/2 cups prepared Thai peanut sauce
- 1 large tomato, diced
- 4 green onions, diced
- 2 pounds cooked shrimp, peeled and
- deveined

DIRECTIONS

Step 1

Add rice vermicelli into boiling water and cook for about five minutes or until done.

Step 2

Combine this rice with tomato, peanut sauce, green onions and shrimp very thoroughly in a medium sized bowl before refrigerating for at least eight hours.

SUMMER TERIYAKI LIME SALAD

Prep Time: 30 mins - **Total Time:** 3 hrs 50 mins

SERVINGS: 6

NUTRITIONAL VALUE

Calories 467 kcal, Fat 31.7 g, Carbohydrates 22.5g, Protein 26.3 g, Cholesterol 54 mg, Sodium 2966 mg

INGREDIENTS

- 4 skinless, boneless chicken breast halves
- 4 cloves garlic
- 1 C. orange juice
- 2 heads romaine lettuce
- 1 C. soy sauce
- 2 tomatoes, chopped
- 1 (12 fluid oz) can or bottle lemon-lime
- 1/3 C. mozzarella cheese
- flavored carbonated beverage
- 1/4 C. grated Parmesan cheese
- 1 lemon, juiced
- 3/4 C. vegetable oil
- 1 tsp salt
- 1/2 tsp ground black pepper

DIRECTIONS

Step 1

Get a large mixing bowl: Stir in it the chicken with the orange juice, soy sauce and lemon-lime carbonated beverage. Place it in the fridge for 2 h to an overnight.

Step 2

Get a small bowl: Mix in it the lemon juice, vegetable oil, salt, pepper and garlic cloves. Place it in the fridge until ready to use.

Step 3

Before you do anything preheat the grill and grease it.

Step 4

Cook the chicken breasts on the grill for 7 to 10 min on each side.

Step 5

Discard the garlic from the dressing. Cut the grilled chicken breasts into strips.

Step 6

Toss the chicken with lettuce, tomatoes, mozzarella, Parmesan in a large serving bowl. Drizzle the marinade on top then serve it right away.

Step 7

Enjoy.

HOW TO MAKE JAPANESE STYLE TERIYAKI SAUCE

Prep Time: 5 mins - **Total Time:** 10 mins

SERVINGS: 4

NUTRITIONAL VALUE

Calories 57 kcal, Fat 0 g, Carbohydrates 7.4g, Protein 1.1 g, Cholesterol 0 mg, Sodium 902 mg

INGREDIENTS

- 1/4 C. dark soy sauce
- 1/4 C. sake
- 2 tbsps mirin (Japanese sweet wine)
- 1 tbsp white sugar

DIRECTIONS

Step 1

Get a bowl mix: sugar, soy sauce, mirin, and sake.

Step 2

Work everything by hand until it is completely smooth and uniform.

Step 3

Place the sauce in the fridge until it is cold.

Step 4

Enjoy.

ROASTED SWEET SOY TERIYAKI CHICKEN

Prep Time: 20 mins - **Total Time:** 6 hrs

SERVINGS: 6

NUTRITIONAL VALUE

Calories 604 kcal, Fat 34.2 g, Carbohydrates 27.9g, Protein 44.3 g, Cholesterol 170 mg, Sodium 1963 mg

INGREDIENTS

- 1 (3 lb) whole chicken, cut in half
- 1 tbsp grated fresh ginger
- 3/4 C. granulated sugar
- 2 cloves garlic, minced
- 3/4 C. soy sauce

DIRECTIONS

Step 1

Clean the chicken pieces and dry them. Place them in casserole dish with there cut side facing the bottom.

Step 2

Get a mixing bowl: Whisk in it the remaining ingredients. Drizzle the mix all over the chicken and place a pieces of plastic. Place it in the fridge for 4 h.

Step 3

Drain the chicken pieces from the marinade and place them on a roasting dish.

Step 4

Before you do anything set the oven to 350 F.

Step 5

Cook the chicken in the oven for 1 h 3 min while basting it with the marinade every 20

min.

Step 6

Enjoy.

JAPANESE BROCCOLI FLORETS ROAST

Prep Time: 8 mins - **Total Time:** 20 mins

SERVINGS: 4

NUTRITIONAL VALUE

Calories 50.9, Fat 0.4g , Cholesterol 0.0mg , Sodium 214.2mg , Carbohydrates 9.9g , Protein 3.9g

INGREDIENTS

- 500 g broccoli, cut into florets
- fresh ground black pepper
- 4 garlic cloves, chopped

- olive oil flavored cooking spray
- 1 tbsp teriyaki sauce

DIRECTIONS

Step 1

Before you do anything preheat the oven to the hottest setting. Cover a baking sheet with some parchment paper.

Step 2

Clean the broccoli with cold water, drain it and pat it dry.

Step 3

Get a large mixing bowl: Toss in it the broccoli with garlic, teriyaki sauce, a pinch of salt and pepper.

Step 4

Spread the mix on the lined up baking sheet. Roast the broccoli in the oven for 7 min. Flip the broccoli florets and cook them for another 7 min then serve it warm.

Step 5

Enjoy.

TASTY TERIYAKI BEEF MEATBALLS

Prep Time: 10 mins - **Total Time:** 35 mins

SERVINGS: 6

NUTRITIONAL VALUE

Calories 174.8, Fat 11.3g , Cholesterol 51.4mg , Sodium 510.6mg , Carbohydrates 2.2g , Protein 14.8g

INGREDIENTS

- 1 lb ground beef

- 1/2 tsp grated gingerroot (optional)
- 1/4 C. teriyaki sauce
- garlic salt
- 2 green onions, chopped

DIRECTIONS

Step 1

Before you do anything preheat the oven to 350 F.

Step 2

Get a large mixing bowl: Combine in it all the ingredients. Mix them well. Shape the mix into 1 inch meatballs.

Step 3

Place the meatballs on a lined baking sheet. Cook them in the oven for 28 min. Serve them warm.

Step 4

Enjoy.

CLASSIC GRILLED TERIYAKI SALMON

Prep Time: 8 hrs - **Total Time:** 8 hrs 12 mins

SERVINGS: 4

NUTRITIONAL VALUE

Calories 272.8, Fat 5.0g , Cholesterol 52.3mg , Sodium 2845.8mg , Carbohydrates 28.6g , Protein 27.6g

INGREDIENTS

- 1 lb salmon fillet

- 1 C. teriyaki sauce or 1 C. teriyaki
- marinade
- 1/4 C. honey

DIRECTIONS

Step 1

Get a large bag: Place it in the salmon fillets with teriyaki sauce. Seal the bag and shake it to coat.

Step 2

Before you do anything preheat the grill and grease it.

Step 3

Remove the salmon fillets from the marinade. Cook it on the grill with skin side facing up for 4 min.

Step 4

Rotate the fillet on the other side and cook it for another 4 min. Flip the salmon fillet and brush it with honey. Cook it for 7 min then serve it warm.

Step 5

Enjoy

HERBED TERIYAKI POTATO QUARTERS

Prep Time: 10 mins **- Total Time:** 26 mins

SERVINGS: 5

NUTRITIONAL VALUE

Calories 129.9, Fat 2.4g , Cholesterol 6.1mg , Sodium 166.5mg , Carbohydrates 24.7g , Protein 3.0g

INGREDIENTS

- 1 1/2 lbs red skinned new potatoes (tiny
- 1 dash cayenne pepper, to taste
- sized, about 10)
- 1 tsp fresh rosemary, minced (optional)
- 1 tbsp butter or 1 tbsp margarine, cut into
- sour cream, to garnish (optional)
- pieces
- 1 tbsp bottled teriyaki sauce
- 1/4 tsp garlic salt, to taste
- 1/4 tsp italian seasoning, crushed
- 1 dash black pepper, to taste

DIRECTIONS

Step 1

Clean the potatoes and slice them into quarters. Place it in a microwave proof pan.

Step 2

Add to it the remaining ingredients except for the rosemary and mix them. Put on the lid and microwave them for 17 min on high or until the potatoes becomes soft.

Step 3

Stir in the rosemary then serve your potato casserole warm.

Step 4

Enjoy.

ITALIAN CHICKEN BREAST TERIYAKI WITH CASHEW RICE

Prep Time: 5 mins - **Total Time:** 20 mins

SERVINGS: 4

NUTRITIONAL VALUE

Calories 659.9, Fat 30.8g 47, Cholesterol 72.6mg , Sodium 3312.8mg , Carbohydrates 64.0g , Protein 32.4g

INGREDIENTS

- 1 C. teriyaki sauce
- cooked rice (4 servings)
- 3/4 C. pineapple juice
- 1 (4 oz) cans crushed pineapple
- 1/2 C. brown sugar
- 3/4 C. cashew pieces
- 1/2 C. vinegar
- various cooked vegetables, your choice
- 1 tsp garlic powder
- 1/4 C. Worcestershire sauce
- 1/2 C. Italian salad dressing
- 1 -1 1/2 lb boneless chicken breast

DIRECTIONS

Step 1

Place a medium saucepan over medium heat: Stir in it the teriyaki sauce with brown sugar, vinegar, pineapple juice, Worcestershire sauce, Italian salad dressing and garlic powder.

Step 2

Cook them until they start boiling to make the marinade.

Step 3

Get a large zip lock bag: Pour in it half of the marinade with the chicken breasts. Seal the bag and shake it to coat. Place it in the fridge for an overnight.

Step 4

Before you do anything preheat the grill and grease it.

Step 5

Cook the rice according to the directions on the package.

Step 6

Drain the chicken and grill the chicken breasts for 8 to 10 min on each side.

Step 7

Get a large mixing bowl: Toss the pineapple with 3/4 C. of cashews and rice.

Step 8

Pour the reserved half of the marinade in a small saucepan. Heat for 5 min.

Step 9

Serve your grilled chicken with the pineapple rice and teriyaki sauce.

Step10

Enjoy.

GLAZED AND GRILLED TERIYAKI SWORDFISH

Prep Time: 15 mins - **Total Time:** 3 hrs 15 mins

SERVINGS: 4

NUTRITIONAL VALUE

Calories 304.9, Fat 13.8g , Cholesterol 66.3mg , Sodium 1533.6mg , Carbohydrates 7.3g , Protein 36.0g

INGREDIENTS

- 2 tbsp canola oil
- 1/4 honey
- 1/4 C. chopped white onion
- 4 (6 oz) center cut swordfish steaks
- 2 -3 minced garlic cloves
- 1 1/2 tsp grated fresh ginger
- 1/2 C. teriyaki sauce

DIRECTIONS

Step 1

Place a saucepan over medium heat. Heat the oil in it. Cook in it the onion, garlic and ginger for 4 min.

Step 2

Stir in the honey with teriyaki sauce. Cook them until they start boiling while stirring all the time. Lower the heat and cook them for 3 min.

Step 3

Place the sauce aside to lose heat. Reserve 1/4 of the sauce.

Step 4

Get a large zip lock bag: Place in it the remaining sauce with swordfish steaks. Seal the bag and shake it to coat. Place it in the fridge for 2 h 30.

Step 5

Before you do anything preheat the grill for 6 min and grease it.

Step 6

Drain the swordfish from the sauce. Cook the swordfish steaks in the grill for 5 min on each side.

Step 7

Remove the steaks from the grill and spray them with a cooking spray. Wipe the grill clean.

Step 8

Cook the swordfish for 4 min on each side with basting them with the reserved sauce. Serve your swordfish steaks warm.

Step 9

Enjoy.

www.ingramcontent.com/pod-product-compliance
Lightning Source LLC
LaVergne TN
LVHW082248150826
845677LV00009B/1565

* 9 7 9 8 4 3 6 6 2 2 3 1 6 *